For Marcia

Tree Crazy

by
Tracy Gallup

Mackinac Island Press

for the love of reading

Once I read a poem about

the leaping greenly spirits of trees.

I wonder if trees have spirits.

Recently we moved into an old house.

We hear noise inside the walls.

My dad thinks it's nesting animals,

but my brother and I

are afraid it is ghosts.

Is the tree calling out to us?

My brother and I climb

up high into its branches.

We pretend we are birds and squirrels

nesting in its sheltering arms.

A man from the city tells us

our talking tree is

two hundred and fifty years old.

He says it is hollow inside

and needs to be cut down.

That night I dream

I am in a forest.

Colors dance around me.

I see acorns with life

waiting inside them,

and falling oak leaves

that look like hands,

beckoning.

Our tree speaks to me

one more time.

Now the talking tree is gone.

I reach for something

in my pocket.

I know what to do.

When a tree speaks to me,

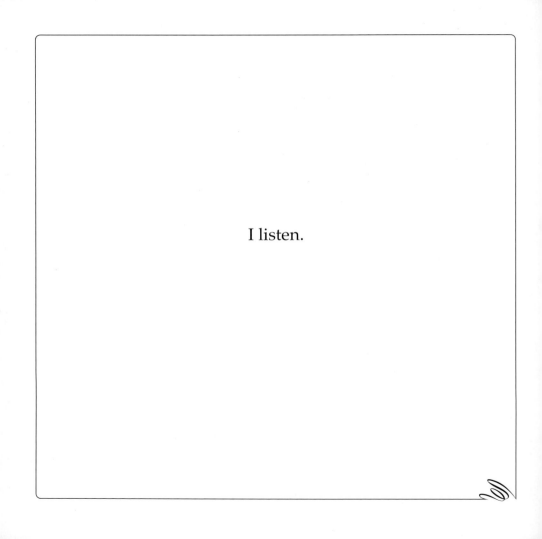

I listen.

Library of Congress
Cataloging-in-Publication Data on file

Tracy Gallup
A Crazy Little Series™: *Tree Crazy*

ISBN 978-1-934133-27-9
Fiction

10 9 8 7 6 5 4 3 2 1

A Mackinac Island Press, Inc. publication
www.mackinacislandpress.com

Mackinac Island Press
for the love of reading

Printed in China